AF270463

ANDRE THE GIANT

A&D Xtreme
BOLD HI-LO NONFICTION

An imprint of Abdo Publishing
abdobooks.com

ALEX MONNIG

TAKE IT TO THE XTREME!

GET READY FOR AN EXTREME ADVENTURE!
THE PAGES OF THIS BOOK WILL TAKE YOU INTO
THE THRILLING WORLD OF PROFESSIONAL WRESTLING.
WHEN YOU HAVE FINISHED READING THIS BOOK, TAKE THE
XTREME CHALLENGE ON PAGE 45 ABOUT WHAT YOU'VE LEARNED!

ABDOBOOKS.COM

Published by Abdo Publishing, a division of ABDO, PO Box 398166, Minneapolis, Minnesota 55439.
Copyright © 2024 by Abdo Consulting Group, Inc. International copyrights reserved in all countries.
No part of this book may be reproduced in any form without written permission from the publisher.
A&D Xtreme™ is a trademark and logo of Abdo Publishing.
Printed in the United States of America, North Mankato, MN.
052023
092023

Design: Kelly Doudna, Mighty Media, Inc.
Production: Mighty Media, Inc.
Editor: Katherine Chu
Cover Photograph: Adam Scull/MediaPunch/IPx/AP Images
Interior Photographs: Adam Scull/Alamy Photo, pp. 4–5; Adam Scull/AP Images, p. 17; Allstar Picture
    Library Limited./Alamy Photo, pp. 24–25; anek.soowannaphoom/Shutterstock Images, pp. 10–11;
    Bettmann/Getty Images, pp. 40–41; CelebrityArchaeology.com/Alamy Photo, pp. 34–35; Claude
    villetaneuse/Wikimedia Commons, pp. 6–7; Ethan/Flickr, p. 31; filo/iStockphoto, p. 16; Jeff
    Goode/Getty Images, pp. 28–29; Jerry Driendl/Getty Images, pp. 30–31; John McKeon/Flickr,
    pp. 18–19; Marty Lederhandler/AP Images, pp. 1, 26–27; MediaPunch/AP Images, pp. 36–37;
    Miguel Discart/Flickr, pp. 42–43; Paul Natkin/Getty Images, pp. 38–39; Pictorial Press Ltd/Alamy
    Photo, pp. 22–23; ProDesign studio/Shutterstock Images, pp. 14–15; Ray Stubblebine/AP Images,
    pp. 20–21; Southtownboy Studio/Shutterstock Images, pp. 12–13; The Stanley Weston Archive/
    Getty Images, pp. 32–33, 44; Wikimedia Commons, pp. 11, 13, 15; William Perugini/Shutterstock
    Images, pp. 8–9
Design Elements: amgun/Shutterstock Images (perspective); sanchesnet1/iStockphoto (spikes color,
    bolts); Wth/Shutterstock Images (stripes)

LIBRARY OF CONGRESS CONTROL NUMBER: 2022948816

PUBLISHER'S CATALOGING-IN-PUBLICATION DATA
Names: Monnig, Alex, author.
Title: Andre the Giant / by Alex Monnig
Description: Minneapolis, Minnesota : Abdo Publishing, 2024 | Series: Xtreme wrestling royalty |
    Includes online resources and index.
Identifiers: ISBN 9781098291457 (lib. bdg.) | ISBN 9781098277918 (ebook)
Subjects: LCSH: Roussimoff, André René, 1946-1993--Juvenile literature. | Wrestlers--Biography--
    Juvenile literature. | Actors--Biography--Juvenile literature. | World Wrestling Entertainment,
    Inc--Juvenile literature.
Classification: DDC 796.812092--dc23

TABLE OF CONTENTS

CHAPTER 1

A HISTORIC MATCH

In 1987, two famous wrestling stars fought at WrestleMania III. Andre the Giant was 7 foot 4 inches (2.2 m) and 500 pounds (226.8 kg). He faced Terry "Hulk Hogan" Bollea, a World Wide Wrestling Federation (WWWF) Champion. The announcer called Andre the Giant "an **immovable** object" and Hogan "an **irresistible** force." This match would go down in history.

Terry "Hulk Hogan" Bollea (*right*) and Andre the Giant fighting during WrestleMania III. The World Wide Wrestling Federation called WrestleMania III the biggest event in the history of sports entertainment.

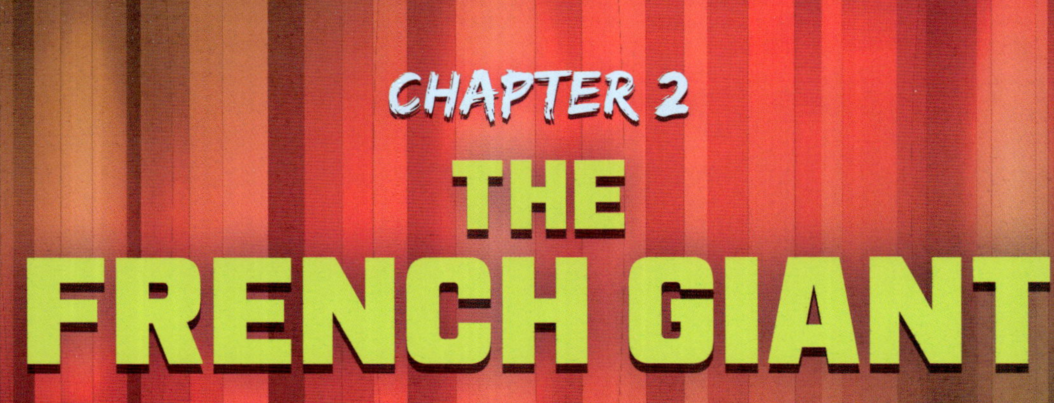

CHAPTER 2
THE FRENCH GIANT

André René Roussimoff was born on May 19, 1946, in France. He was born with acromegaly, a condition also known as giantism. It meant André had more growth **hormones** in his body than the average person. So, he grew bigger and faster than most people.

While living in Paris, France, André also worked as a furniture mover because of his size and strength.

André grew up on his family's farm in Moliens, France. After finishing school at age 14, he worked at a factory in a nearby town. There, he met boxer Robert Lageat. After seeing how large André was, Lageat offered to train him as a professional wrestler in Paris, France.

During his late teens, André joined Lageat's gym in Paris. He trained with other wrestlers and learned different wrestling moves. André made his official wrestling **debut** in January 1966. He was a huge success!

Daniel "the Little Prince" Dubail was a famous French wrestler in the late 1960s. In 1966, he wrestled against André.

XTREME FACT

André was given the nickname Jean Ferré in honor of the French folk hero Grand Ferré. He was a peasant from Rivecourt, France, who **defended** a castle against the English.

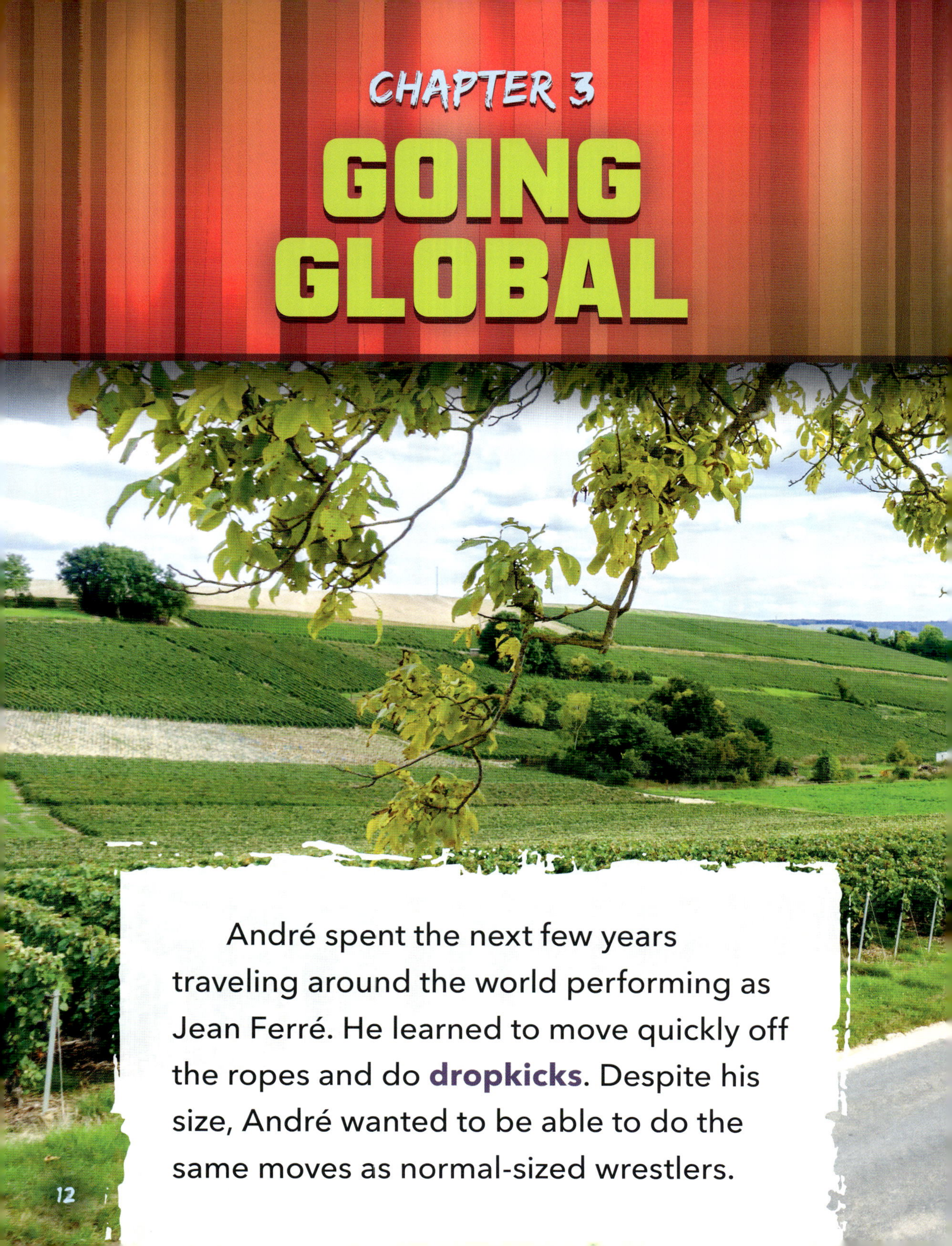

CHAPTER 3

GOING GLOBAL

André spent the next few years traveling around the world performing as Jean Ferré. He learned to move quickly off the ropes and do **dropkicks**. Despite his size, André wanted to be able to do the same moves as normal-sized wrestlers.

André wrestled as Jean Ferré with Édouard Carpentier (*left*) and Yvon Robert (*right*). André met Carpentier when André moved a tree blocking Carpentier's car in France.

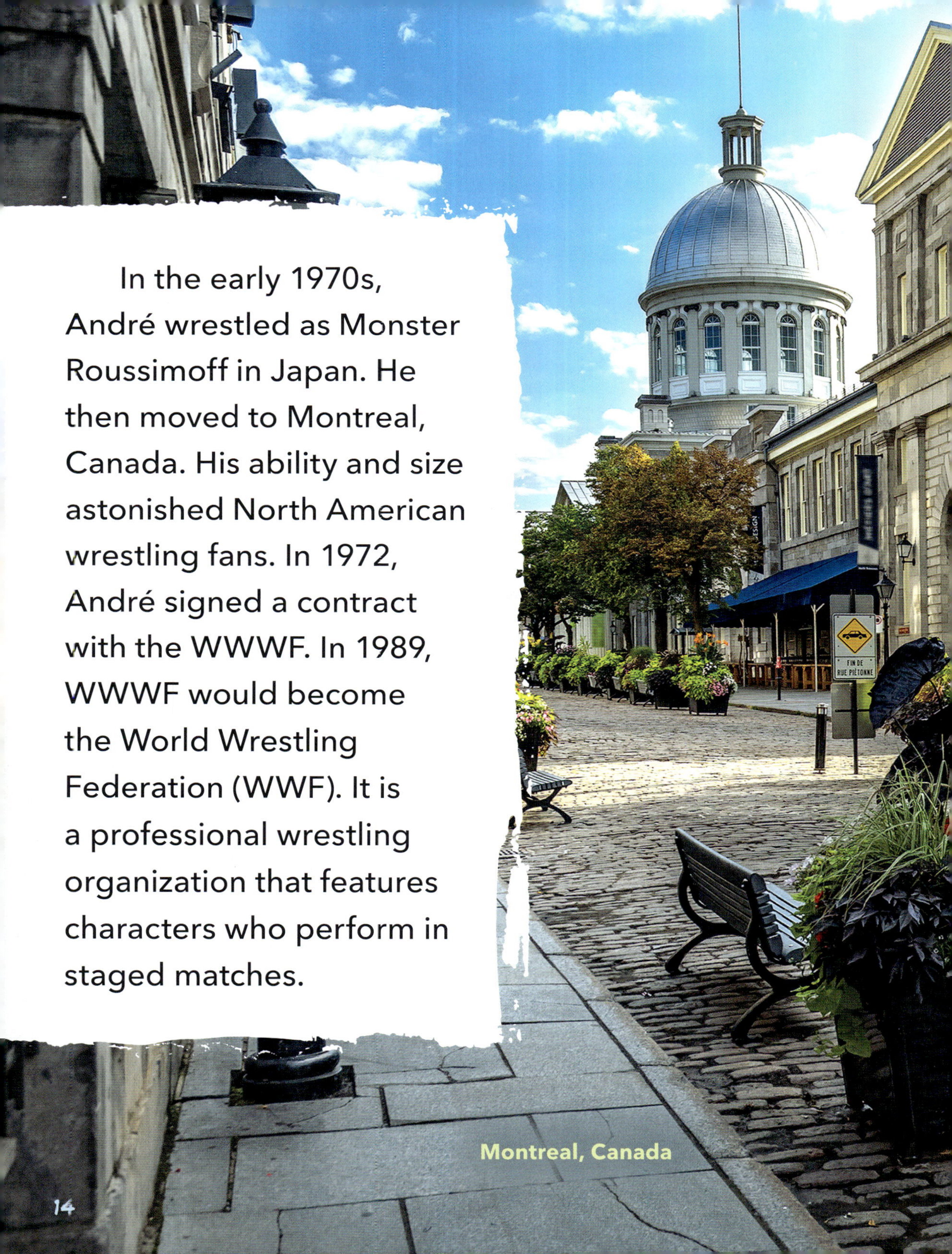

In the early 1970s, André wrestled as Monster Roussimoff in Japan. He then moved to Montreal, Canada. His ability and size astonished North American wrestling fans. In 1972, André signed a contract with the WWWF. In 1989, WWWF would become the World Wrestling Federation (WWF). It is a professional wrestling organization that features characters who perform in staged matches.

Andre the Giant
using the Destroyer
move in 1973

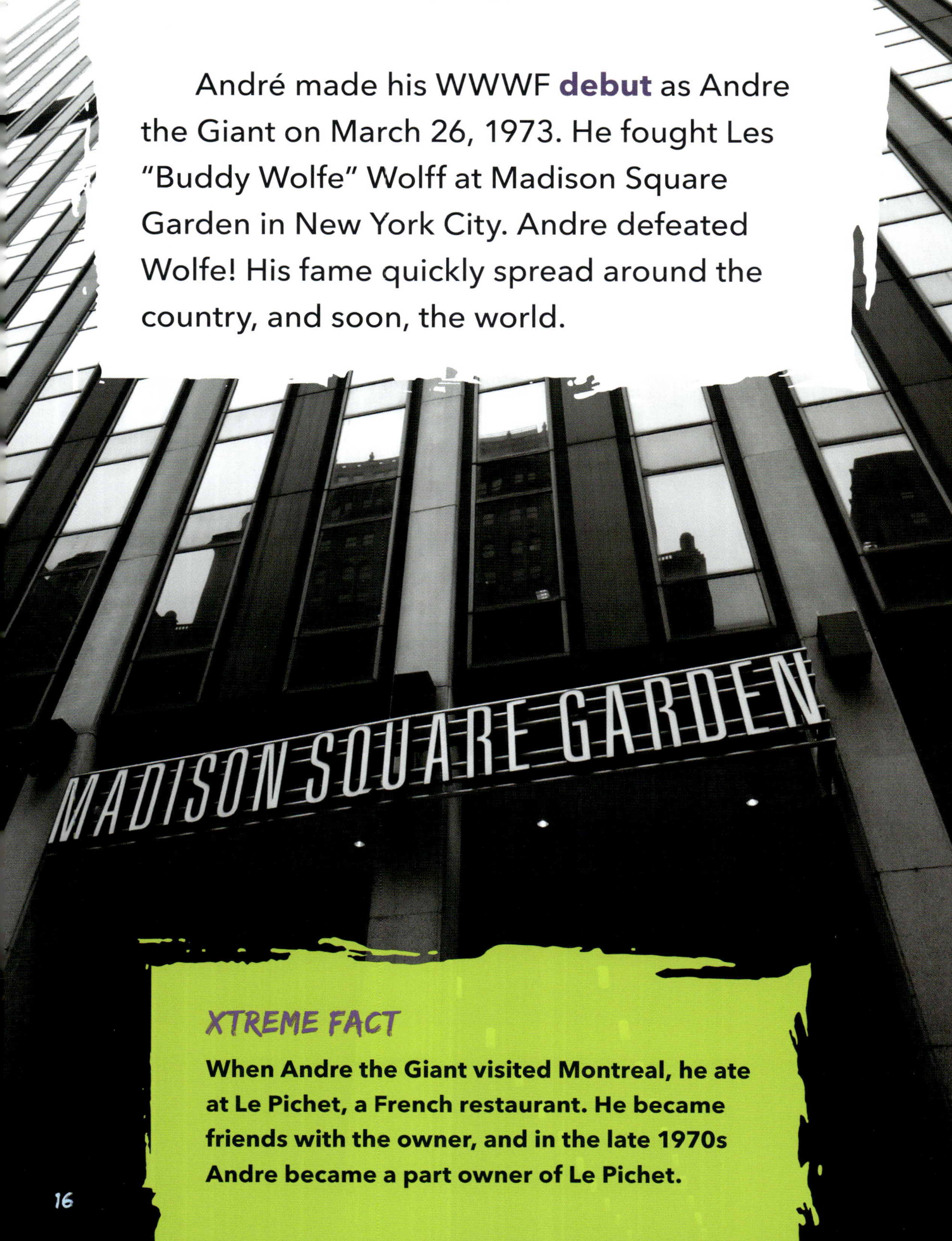

André made his WWWF **debut** as Andre the Giant on March 26, 1973. He fought Les "Buddy Wolfe" Wolff at Madison Square Garden in New York City. Andre defeated Wolfe! His fame quickly spread around the country, and soon, the world.

XTREME FACT

When Andre the Giant visited Montreal, he ate at Le Pichet, a French restaurant. He became friends with the owner, and in the late 1970s Andre became a part owner of Le Pichet.

WrestleMania I was also held at Madison Square Garden in 1985. Andre the Giant defeated John "Big John Studd" Minton (*right*) with a body slam.

CHAPTER 4

BECOMING A LEGEND

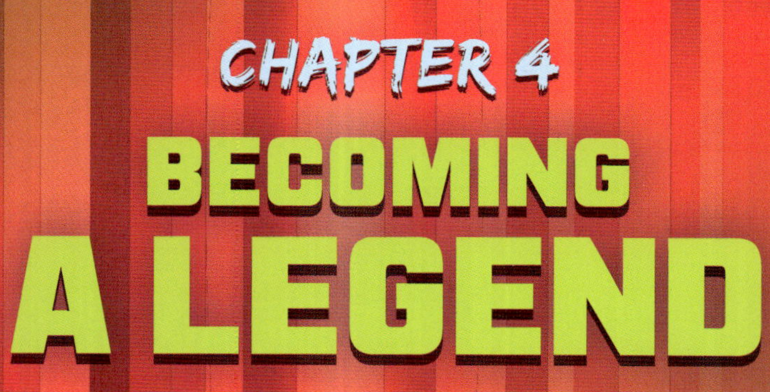

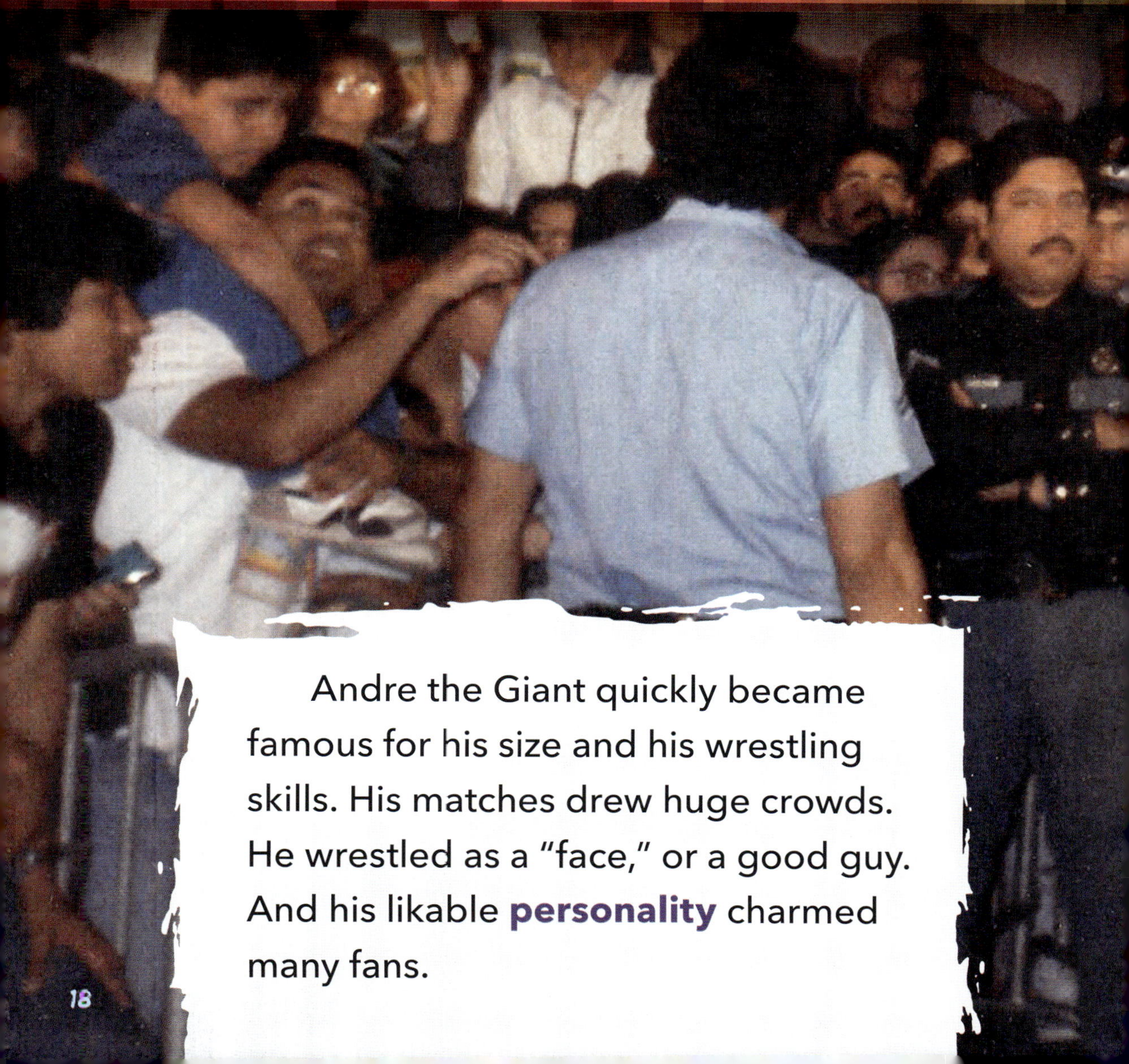

Andre the Giant quickly became famous for his size and his wrestling skills. His matches drew huge crowds. He wrestled as a "face," or a good guy. And his likable **personality** charmed many fans.

Andre the Giant during a *WWF Superstars of Wrestling* taping in the late 1980s. At that time, *WWF Superstars of Wrestling* was the WWF's biggest broadcast TV show.

During the match's initial rounds, Chuck Wepner (*back to camera*) tapped Andre the Giant with punches. But Andre ended the match after Wepner punched him hard in the third round.

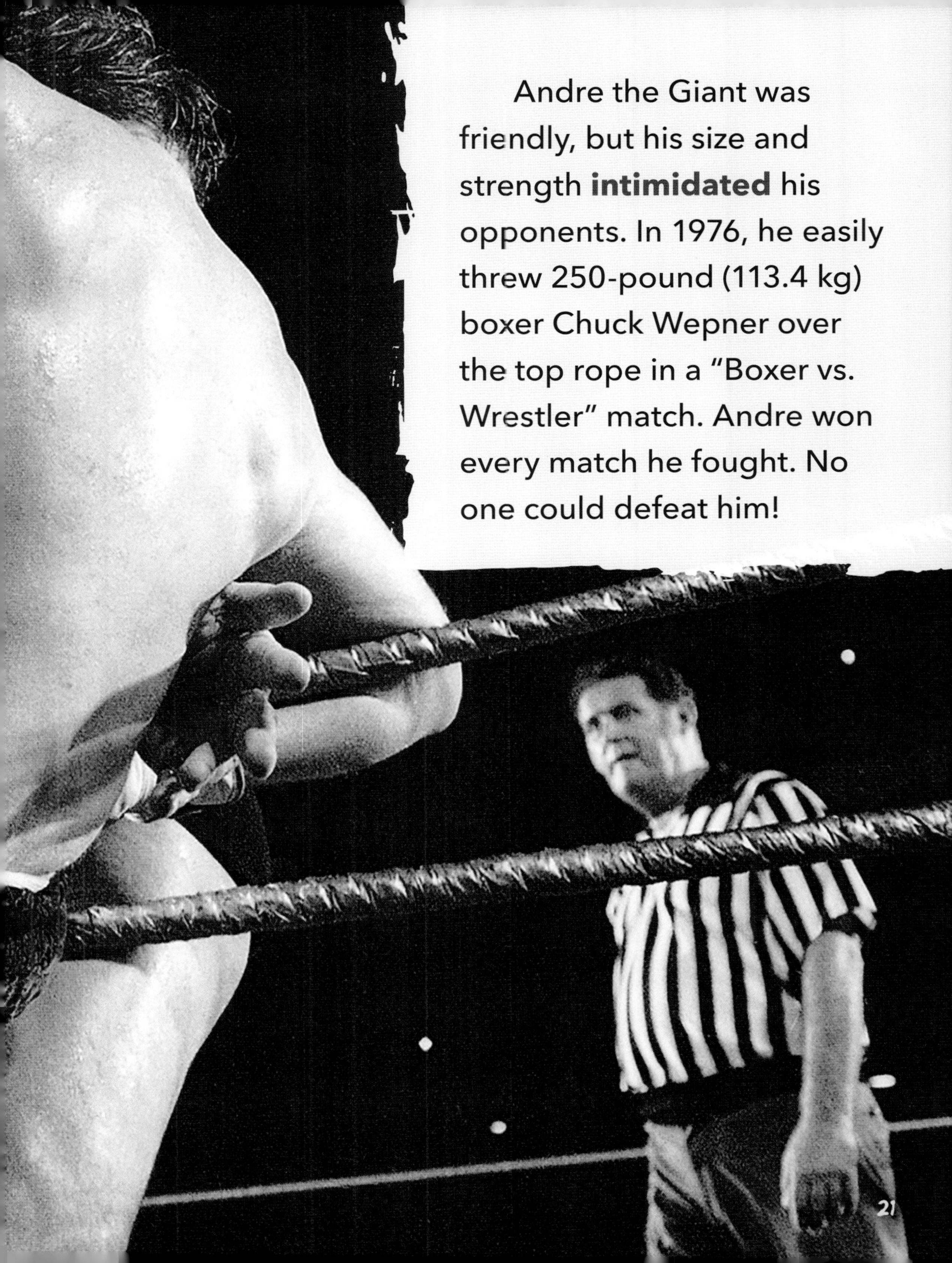

Andre the Giant was friendly, but his size and strength **intimidated** his opponents. In 1976, he easily threw 250-pound (113.4 kg) boxer Chuck Wepner over the top rope in a "Boxer vs. Wrestler" match. Andre won every match he fought. No one could defeat him!

One of Andre the Giant's rivals was Randall "'Macho Man' Randy Savage" Poffo (*center*). Savage successfully defended his championship title against Andre.

Andre the Giant towered over his opponents, controlling each fight. His famous moves defeated many wrestlers. One was the Sitdown Splash. Andre would drop into a seated position on his fallen opponent's chest. He was also known for his double underhook suplex move. Andre would hook his arms under his opponent's arms. Then he would fall back, flipping his opponent over his head.

XTREME FACT

One of Andre the Giant's nicknames was "the Eighth Wonder of the World." It was based on the giant gorilla in the classic movie *King Kong*.

CHAPTER 5

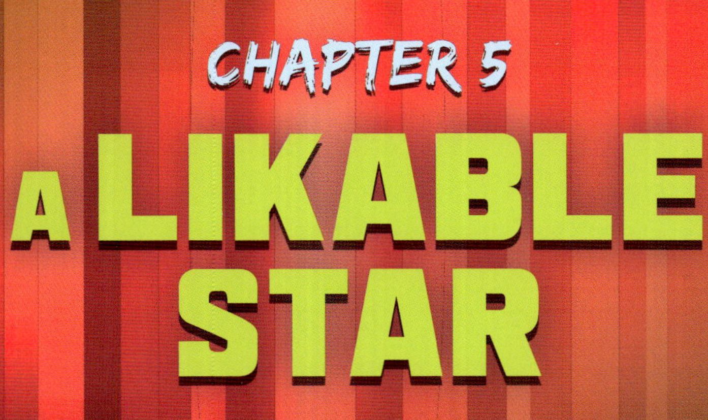

A LIKABLE STAR

Professional wrestling gained popularity across the US in the 1980s. As one of the WWWF's biggest stars, Andre the Giant was a big reason for this. Many fans loved to watch him win matches.

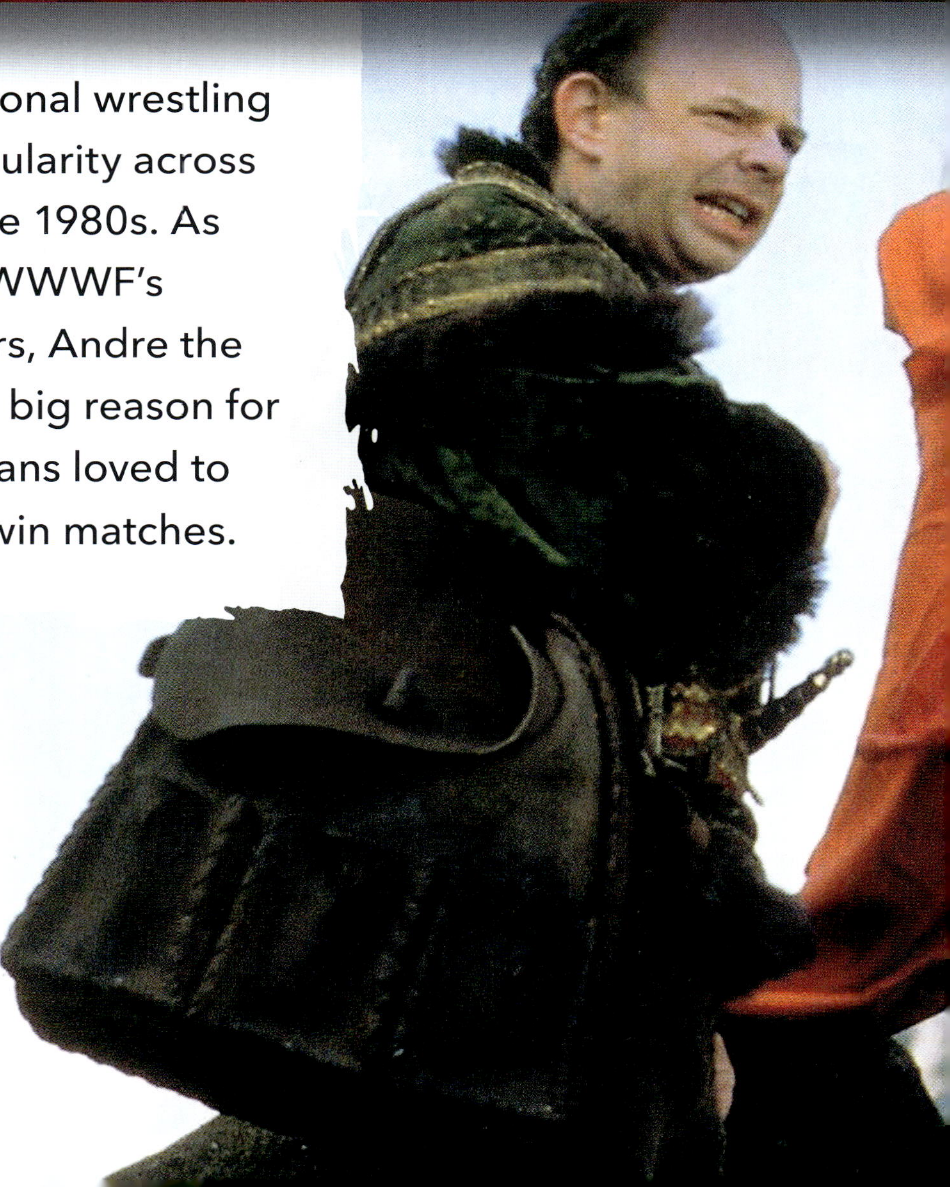

His popularity also earned him appearances on TV shows and in films. His most famous acting role was as a giant in the 1987 film *The Princess Bride.*

Andre the Giant comparing fist sizes with Chuck Wepner. Andre's hands were so large many who met him would compare their hands or heads with his hands.

Andre the Giant's good nature helped him become famous. He was known for being generous. He would pay the dinner bill when going out with friends. He also became friends outside the ring with opponents he liked.

Andre the Giant had plenty of **memorable** moments in his career. Many of them included Hulk Hogan. The two were rivals and friends in multiple **iconic** matches. Many fans considered them to be two of the best wrestlers of all time.

Andre the Giant argues with the referee during a 1989 match against Jake "the Snake" Roberts. In the end, Andre won the match.

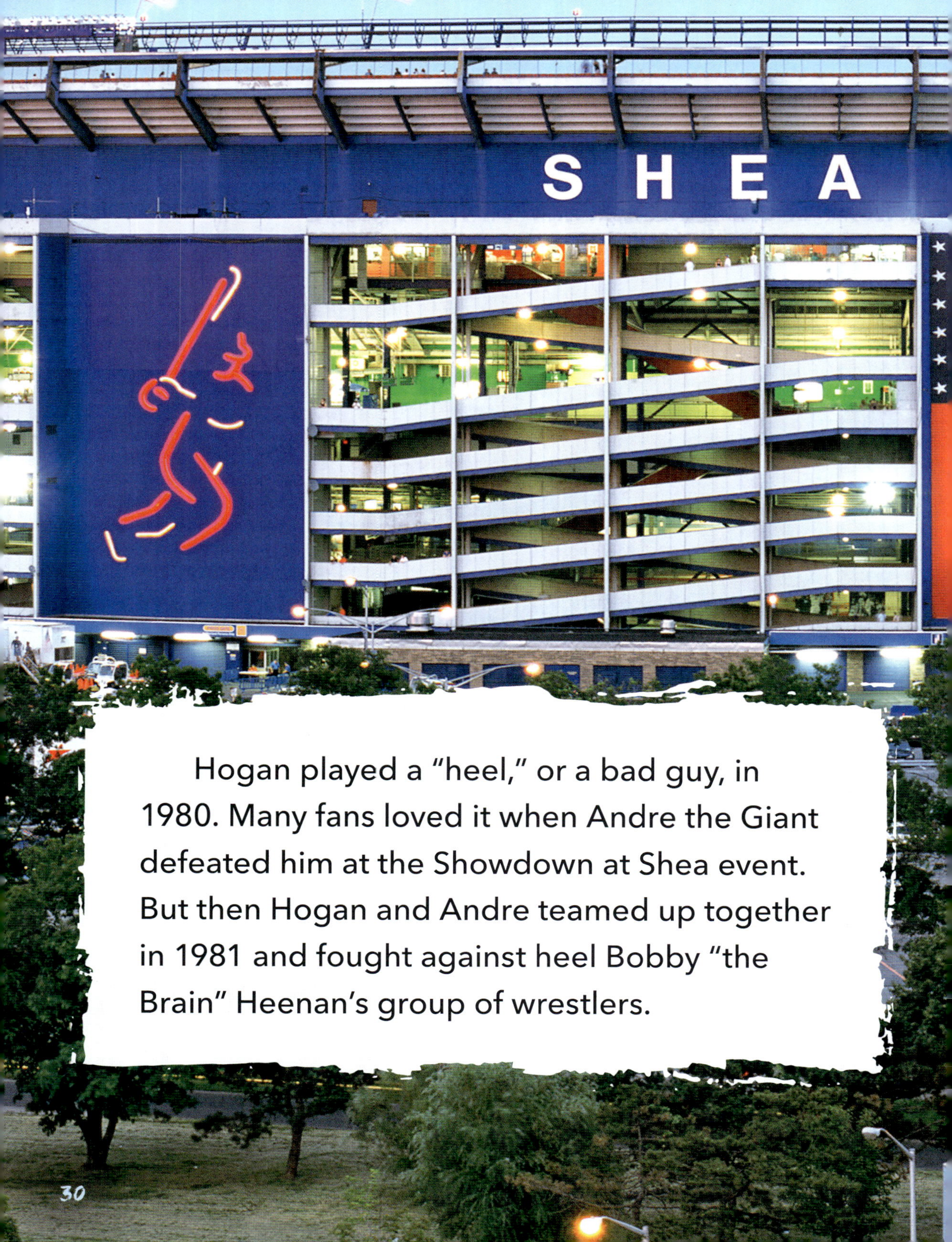

Hogan played a "heel," or a bad guy, in 1980. Many fans loved it when Andre the Giant defeated him at the Showdown at Shea event. But then Hogan and Andre teamed up together in 1981 and fought against heel Bobby "the Brain" Heenan's group of wrestlers.

Andre the Giant (*second from right*) giving one of Bobby Heenan's wrestlers Christopher "King Kong Bundy" Pallies (*center*) his "size 20 boot" during a tag-team match in New York in 1985

CHAPTER 7

FROM FRIEND TO RIVAL

Many fans loved Andre the Giant and Hogan's friendship. But it ended in 1987. Hogan received a trophy for reaching three years as WWWF Champion. Andre also received a trophy for never losing an official match for 15 years. But Hogan's trophy was larger than Andre's. This bothered Andre.

In 1980, Andre the Giant faced Hogan (*right*) during a wrestling event in Montreal, Canada.

Hogan and Andre the Giant fight during WrestleMania III. Their first fight against each other was in 1978 when Hogan went by the name "Terry Boulder."

XTREME FACT

Terry "Hulk Hogan" Bolea might be Andre the Giant's most famous wrestling partner. But Andre also teamed up with Tonga "Haku" Fifita, Virgil "Dusty Rhodes" Runnels, and Ted "the Million Dollar Man" DiBiase.

Andre the Giant was so upset he joined Heenan. He also challenged Hogan to a match for the championship. The two would fight for the championship belt at WrestleMania III. This was the WWWF's most important and popular annual event.

XTREME FACT

Andre the Giant beat Hogan in February 1988, winning the WWWF Championship for the first and only time.

Andre the Giant lifting Hogan during the February 1988 Saturday Night Main Event match. Due to his size and strength, Andre would easily overpower his opponents.

Tens of thousands of fans packed the Pontiac Silverdome in Michigan for WrestleMania III. During the match, Andre the Giant almost **squeezed** the life out of Hogan. But Hogan hit Andre with a move that became known as "the **body slam** heard 'round the world." Hogan won the fight, ending Andre's 15-year undefeated **streak**. Many critics consider this **iconic** match to be one of the most important in wrestling history.

CHAPTER 8

HEALTH AND DEATH

Andre the Giant's enormous body helped make him wrestling royalty. But he lived most of his life in pain because of his acromegaly. As Andre aged, the pain worsened. But he continued to perform for his fans.

Andre the Giant (*far left*) faced multiple opponents during a Battle Royal match at WrestleMania II in 1986. He defeated all the other wrestlers, winning the match.

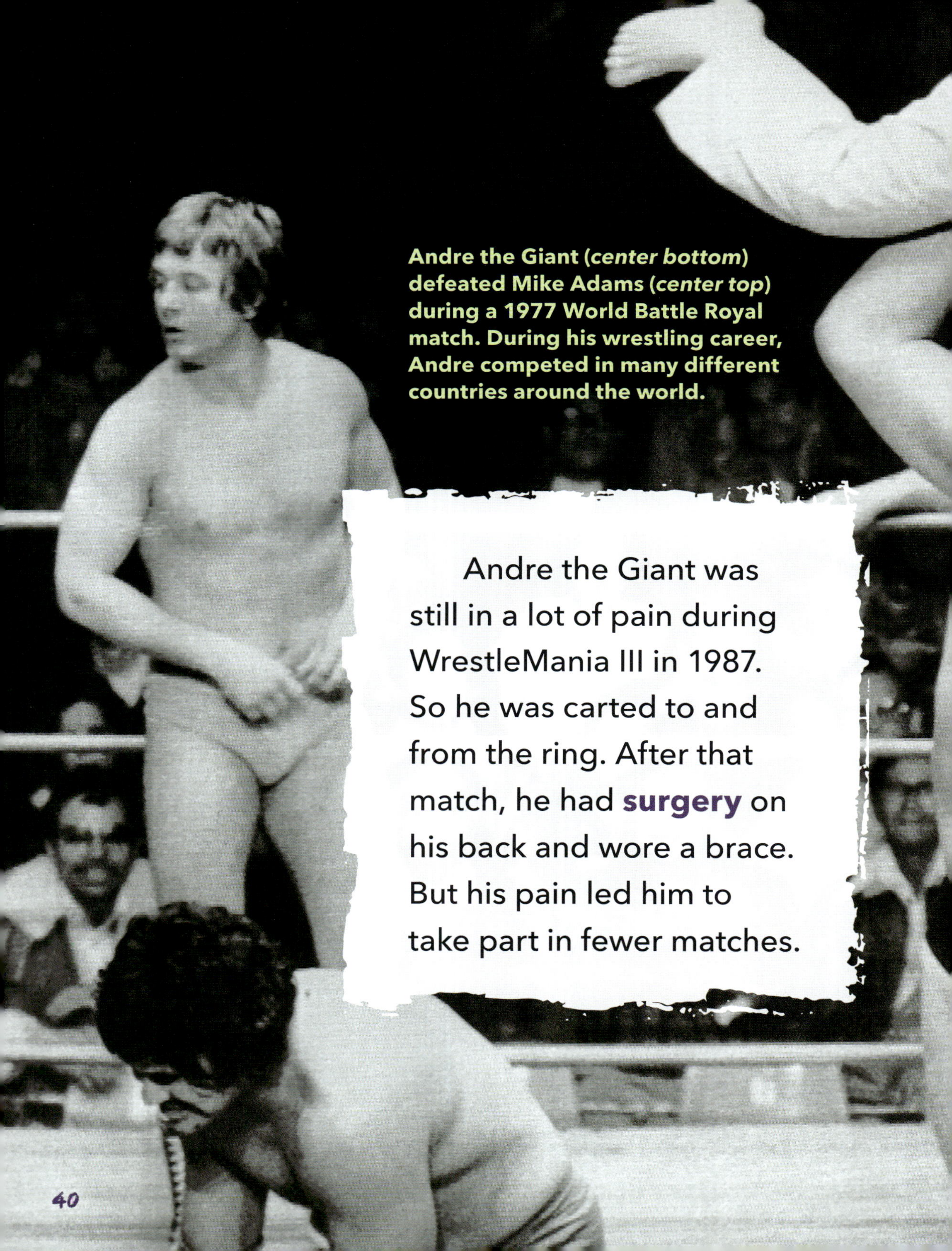

Andre the Giant was still in a lot of pain during WrestleMania III in 1987. So he was carted to and from the ring. After that match, he had **surgery** on his back and wore a brace. But his pain led him to take part in fewer matches.

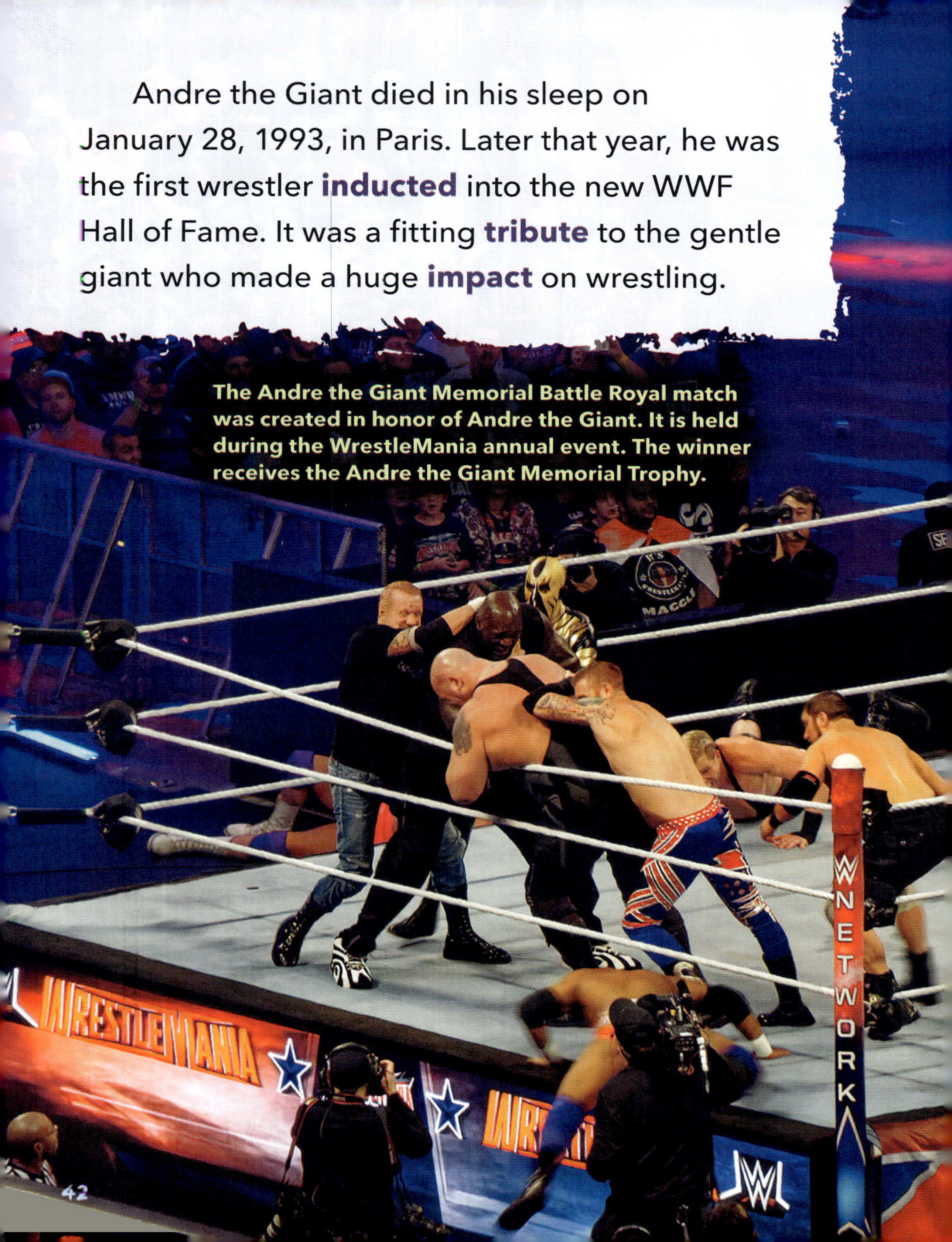

Andre the Giant died in his sleep on January 28, 1993, in Paris. Later that year, he was the first wrestler **inducted** into the new WWF Hall of Fame. It was a fitting **tribute** to the gentle giant who made a huge **impact** on wrestling.

The Andre the Giant Memorial Battle Royal match was created in honor of Andre the Giant. It is held during the WrestleMania annual event. The winner receives the Andre the Giant Memorial Trophy.

XTREME FACT

Andre the Giant left his parents' farm in his late teens. But he still enjoyed the ranch lifestyle. When he wasn't wrestling, he spent his time on his farm in North Carolina.

CHAPTER 9

LARGER THAN LIFE

Andre the Giant's size was matched by his smile and positive **attitude**. His condition caused his career to be cut short. But his larger-than-life **personality** lives on. He is remembered as a beloved wrestler with a big heart.

XTREME CHALLENGE

1) Would you rather be a smaller, quicker wrestler or a larger, slower wrestler?

2) What country was Andre the Giant born in?

3) Andre's giantism caused his body to hurt. What other issues do you think he experienced living with the condition?

4) What boxer did Andre throw over the ropes in 1976?

5) What popular movie did Andre play the role of a giant in?

GLOSSARY

attitude—the way you think or feel about something.

body slam—a wrestling throw in which the opponent's body is lifted and brought down hard to the mat.

debut—a first appearance.

defend—to protect from harm or attack.

dropkick—an attack where the wrestler jumps up and kicks the opponent with the soles of both feet.

hormone—something created by one kind of cell that moves through the body and affects other cells.

iconic—widely known and acknowledged especially for distinctive excellence.

immovable—not able to be moved.

impact—having a powerful influence on.

induct—to admit as a member.

intimidate—to make timid or fearful.

irresistible—impossible to resist.

memorable—worth remembering, or easy to remember.

personality—the special characteristics of a person.

squeeze—to press or grip something tightly.

streak—a consecutive series.

surgery—the treating of sickness or injury by cutting into and repairing body parts.

tribute—something that is done, given, or performed to show appreciation, respect, or affection.

ONLINE RESOURCES

To learn more about Andre the Giant, please visit **abdobooklinks.com** or scan this QR code. These links are routinely monitored and updated to provide the most current information available.

INDEX